Quotes to
Seize the Day

CARPE
DIEM

edited by
Linda Picone

FALL RIVER PRESS

New York

FALL RIVER PRESS

New York

An Imprint of Sterling Publishing Co., Inc.
1166 Avenue of the Americas
New York, NY 10036

© 2016 by Linda Picone

ISBN 978-1-4351-6266-2

Distributed in Canada by Sterling Publishing Co., Inc.
Canadian Manda Group, 664 Annette Street
Toronto, Ontario, Canada M6S 2C8
Distributed in the United Kingdom by GMC Distribution Services
Castle Place, 166 High Street, Lewes, East Sussex, England BN7 1XU
Distributed in Australia by Capricorn Link (Australia) Pty. Ltd.
P.O. Box 704, Windsor, NSW 2756, Australia

For information about custom editions, special sales, and premium
and corporate purchases, please contact Sterling Special Sales at
800-805-5489 or specialsales@sterlingpublishing.com.

Manufactured in the United States of America

2 4 6 8 10 9 7 5 3 1

www.sterlingpublishing.com

Cover design by David Ter-Avanesyan
Book design by Rich Hazelton

Contents

Introduction

What Does It Mean to Seize the Day?

FOR MANY OF US, THE FIRST TIME WE HEARD THE WORDS *carpe diem* was when Robin Williams, as English teacher John Keating in the movie *Dead Poets Society*, urged his students to "seize the day."

But the original phrase—and sentiment—dates back to roughly 40 BC, when the poet Horace wrote: *Dum loquimur, fugerit invida aetas: carpe diem, quam minimum credula postero.* Or: "While we're talking, envious time is fleeing: pluck the day, put no trust in the future."

Today, of course, we substitute "seize the day" for "pluck the day," but the meaning is the same. The idea is to find maximum happiness in the day in front of you, rather than hoping for something different, something better, in the future—or sighing over the past.

We can think of the phrase in a negative way: why bother planning or hoping for the future when we could be hit by a bus tomorrow? Forget pension plans, buying a house—even having children. Forget eating healthy foods, getting exercise, or giving up bad habits.

But most of us like to think of the phrase as encouraging us to get the most out of every day, to stop and smell the roses, to recognize all the wonderful things we have in our lives that we tend to take for granted.

Think of it as grabbing the day, any day, and squeezing until you experience all the joy of it, no matter what else is going on in your life. Look at that gorgeous sunrise. Listen to the sound of loved ones sleeping. Luxuriate in the hot water of the shower. Taste the first cup of coffee and feel its warmth. Be grateful that you have work you like—or that at least pays the bills. Or be grateful that you don't have to go to a job each day and can simply enjoy free hours seeing friends, walking the dog, reading a favorite book.

It's harder, of course, when times are tough. But even then we can find dozens of ways to experience pleasure and even joy in every day—and sometimes we can be grateful for the tough times that help us discover who we really are and what's important to us.

The quotes in this book remind us to "pluck" or "seize" the day by not taking for granted the wonderful experiences, people, places, and advantages we have, from family to good friends to the natural world and more.

In the words of the band Metallica: "So take this world and shake it. Come squeeze and suck the day. Come carpe diem, baby."

—LINDA PICONE

Through the Eyes of a Child

CHILDREN OFTEN CAN'T WAIT TO GROW UP. THEY MAKE SURE WE know that they are six "and a half," not just six. They look forward to making their own rules. And yet they know how to enjoy each day better than the adults around them.

We adults sometimes long for what we remember as the simple, happy days of childhood, not quite realizing that those days are still within our grasp.

Approach each day and each new experience with childlike wonder. You don't have to be a child to see the world through fresh, unjaded eyes; you just have to decide that's how you want to live.

Sweet childish days, that were as long
As twenty days are now.

—William Wordsworth

We could never have loved the earth so well if we had had
no childhood in it.

—George Eliot

Childhood is the fiery furnace in which we are melted
down to essentials, and that essential shaped for good.

—Katherine Anne Porter

There is always one moment in childhood when the door
opens and lets the future in.

—Graham Greene

Childhood is the world of miracle or of magic: it is as if
creation rose luminously out of the night, all new and
fresh and astonishing.

—Eugene Ionesco

If you carry your childhood with you, you never become older.

—Tom Stoppard

All who remember their childhood remember the strange vague sense, when some new experience came, that every thing else was going to be changed, and that there would be no lapse into the old monotony.

—George Eliot

It is never too late to have a happy childhood.

—Tom Robbins

What we remember from childhood we remember forever—permanent ghosts, stamped, inked, imprinted, eternally seen.

—Cynthia Ozick

The older I grow, the more earnestly I feel that the few joys of childhood are the best that life has to give.

—Ellen Glasgow

Childhood is a short season.

—Helen Hayes

All children have creative power.

—Brenda Ueland

The finest inheritance you can give to a child is to allow it to make its own way, completely on its own feet.

—Isadora Duncan

Only a child sees things with perfect clarity, because it hasn't developed all those filters which prevent us from seeing things that we don't expect to see.

—Douglas Adams

If we could destroy custom at a blow and see the stars as a child sees them, we should need no other apocalypse.

—G.K. Chesterton

Childhood, at its best, is a perpetual adventure, in the truest sense of that overtaxed word: a setting forth into trackless lands that might have come to existence the instant before you first laid eyes on them.

—MICHAEL CHABON

The soul is healed by being with children.

—FYODOR DOSTOEVSKY

All of us have moments in our childhood where we come alive for the first time. And we go back to those moments and think, This is when I became myself.

—RITA DOVE

Children are the living messages we send to a time we will not see.

—JOHN F. KENNEDY

Play is the work of the child.

—MARIA MONTESSORI

Everything is ceremony in the wild garden of childhood.

—PABLO NERUDA

Old age lives minutes slowly, hours quickly; childhood
chews hours and swallows minutes.

—MALCOLM DE CHAZAL

I'd give all wealth that years have piled,
The slow result of Life's decay,
To be once more a little child
For one bright summer-day.

—LEWIS CARROLL

Childhood is measured out by sounds and smells and
sights, before the dark hour of reason grows.

—JOHN BETJEMAN

So the first step out of childhood is made all at once,
without looking before or behind, without caution, and
nothing held in reserve.

—URSULA K. LE GUIN

The eyes of childhood are magnifying lenses.

—EDWARD TELLER

—

Childhood is not from birth to a certain age and at a
    certain age
The child is grown and puts away childish things.
Childhood is the kingdom where nobody dies.

Nobody that matters, that is.

—EDNA ST. VINCENT MILLAY

All in the Family

O NE WAY OR ANOTHER, WE ALL HAVE FAMILIES. WE ARE BORN into families, we may raise our own, or we may create a family through networks of people we aren't related to, but whom we love.

We humans are social animals, and that socialization starts with our families, no matter how they have come together around us. Sometimes families drive us nuts, sometimes they make us angry, sometimes we just want to be alone. But no matter what, we are who we are because of them.

Give a little thanks, silent or otherwise, for the family that surrounds you, whether it's a family related by blood or love or both.

Family is not an important thing. It's everything.

—Michael J. Fox

~

To us, family means putting your arms around each other and being there.

—Barbara Bush

~

A happy family is but an earlier heaven.

—George Bernard Shaw

~

A family is a risky venture, because the greater the love, the greater the loss . . . that's the trade-off. But I'll take it all.

—Brad Pitt

~

My father used to play with my brother and me in the yard. Mother would come out and say, "You're tearing up the grass." "We're not raising grass," Dad would reply. "We're raising boys."

—Harmon Killebrew

We were a strange little band of characters trudging through life sharing diseases and toothpaste, coveting one another's desserts, hiding shampoo, borrowing money, locking each other out of our rooms, inflicting pain and kissing to heal it in the same instant, loving, laughing, defending, and trying to figure out the common thread that bound us all together.

—ERMA BOMBECK

The family—that dear octopus from whose tentacles we never quite escape, nor, in our inmost hearts, ever quite wish to.

—DODIE SMITH

~

Family faces are magic mirrors. Looking at people who belong to us, we see the past, present, and future.

—GAIL LUMET BUCKLEY

~

What can you do to promote world peace? Go home and love your family.

—MOTHER TERESA

~

A family with an old person has a living treasure of gold.

—CHINESE PROVERB

~

Whatever you call it, whoever you are, you need one.

—JANE HOWARD

The family is a haven in a heartless world.

—CHRISTOPHER LASCH

There is an interconnectedness among members that
bonds the family, much like mountain climbers who
rope themselves together when climbing a mountain,
so that if someone should slip or need support, he's held
up by the others until he regains his footing.

—PHIL MCGRAW

In family life, love is the oil that eases friction, the cement
that binds closer together, and the music that brings
harmony.

—FRIEDRICH NIETZSCHE

You can kiss your family and friends goodbye and put
miles between you, but at the same time you carry them
with you in your heart, your mind, your stomach, because
you do not just live in a world but a world lives in you.

—FREDERICK BUECHNER

Family life is full of major and minor crises—the ups and downs of health, success and failure in career, marriage and divorce—and all kinds of characters. It is tied to places and events and histories. With all of these felt details, life etches itself into memory and personality. It's difficult to imagine anything more nourishing to the soul.

—THOMAS MOORE

Rejoice with your family in the beautiful land of life.

—ALBERT EINSTEIN

I sustain myself with the love of family.

—MAYA ANGELOU

It didn't matter how big our house was; it mattered that there was love in it.

—PETER BUFFETT

Your are born into your family and your family is born into you. No returns. No exchanges.

—ELIZABETH BERG

The happiest moments of my life have been the few which I have passed at home in the bosom of my family.

—THOMAS JEFFERSON

You've Got a Friend— or Two or Three

WITH OUR FRIENDS WE LAUGH, CRY ON THEIR SHOULDERS, and celebrate life events, big and small. A good friend will tell you when you're making a mistake—and love you even if you ignore their advice.

Because they're so much a part of our lives, we sometimes take our friends for granted. We don't call when we should, we forget a birthday, we miss the chance to say how much we value them. Friendship, like a hardy plant, thrives even with small doses of attention.

Take just a few minutes each day to touch base with a friend you may not have talked to recently or who needs some extra attention right now. Let them know you care and that you are glad to have them in your life.

I would rather walk with a friend in the dark than alone in the light.

—HELEN KELLER

I cannot even imagine where I would be today were it not for that handful of friends who have given me a heart full of joy. Let's face it, friends make life a lot more fun.

—CHARLES R. SWINDOLL

Friendship is unnecessary, like philosophy, like art. . . . It has no survival value; rather it is one of those things that give value to survival.

—C.S. LEWIS

Sometimes being a friend means mastering the art of timing. There is a time for silence. A time to let go and allow people to hurl themselves into their own destiny. And a time to prepare to pick up the pieces when it's all over.

—GLORIA NAYLOR

In the sweetness of friendship let there be laughter, and
    sharing of pleasures.
For in the dew of little things the heart finds its morning
    and is refreshed.

—KAHLIL GIBRAN

My best friend is the man who in wishing me well wishes
it for my sake.

—ARISTOTLE

It is one of the blessings of old friends that you can afford
to be stupid with them.

—RALPH WALDO EMERSON

In everyone's life, at some time, our inner fire goes out.
It is then burst into flame by an encounter with another
human being. We should all be thankful for those people
who rekindle the inner spirit.

—ALBERT SCHWEITZER

When we honestly ask ourselves which person in our lives means the most to us, we often find that it is those who, instead of giving advice, solutions, or cures, have chosen rather to share our pain and touch our wounds with a warm and tender hand.

—Henri Nouwen

My best friend is the one who brings out the best in me.

—HENRY FORD

Things are never quite as scary when you've got a best friend.

—BILL WATTERSON

Let us be grateful to people who make us happy; they are the charming gardeners who make our souls blossom.

—MARCEL PROUST

The language of friendship is not words but meanings.

—HENRY DAVID THOREAU

There are no strangers here; only friends you haven't yet met.

—WILLIAM BUTLER YEATS

True friends stab you in the front.

—OSCAR WILDE

True friendship is like sound health; the value of it is seldom known until it be lost.

—CHARLES CALEB COLTON

A friend is one who knows you and loves you just the same.

—ELBERT HUBBARD

Friendship is the source of the greatest pleasures, and without friends even the most agreeable pursuits become tedious.

—THOMAS AQUINAS

Instead of loving your enemies, treat your friends a little better.

—E.W. HOWE

Lots of people want to ride with you in the limo, but what you want is someone who will take the bus with you when the limo breaks down.

—OPRAH WINFREY

I have perceiv'd that to be with those I like is enough.

—Walt Whitman

The best time to make friends is before you need them.

—Ethel Barrymore

When a friend is in trouble, don't annoy him by asking if there is anything you can do; think up something appropriate, and do it.

—E.W. Howe

Laughter is not at all a bad beginning for a friendship, and it is far the best ending for one.

—Oscar Wilde

Friendship is born at that moment when one person says to another: "What? You too? I thought I was the only one."

—C.S. Lewis

I think if I've learned anything about friendship, it's to hang in, stay connected, fight for them, and let them fight for you. Don't walk away, don't be distracted, don't be too busy or tired, don't take them for granted. Friends are part of the glue that holds life and faith together. Powerful stuff.

—Jon Katz

The friend who holds your hand and says the wrong thing is made of dearer stuff than the one who stays away.

—Barbara Kingsolver

~

We cannot tell the precise moment when friendship is formed. As in filling a vessel drop by drop, there is at last a drop which makes it run over; so in a series of kindnesses there is at last one which makes the heart run over.

—Ray Bradbury

~

You can make more friends in two months by becoming interested in other people than you can in two years by trying to get other people interested in you.

—Dale Carnegie

~

Do not save your loving speeches
    For your friends till they are dead;
Do not write them on their tombstones,
    Speak them rather now instead.

—Anna Cummins

It's the friends you can call up at 4 a.m. that matter.

—MARLENE DIETRICH

———

How many slams in an old screen door?
  Depends how loud you shut it.
How many slices in a bread?
  Depends how thin you cut it.
How much good inside a day?
  Depends how good you live 'em.
How much love inside a friend?
  Depends how much you give 'em.

—SHEL SILVERSTEIN

———

The most basic and powerful way to connect to another person is to listen. Just listen. Perhaps the most important thing we ever give each other is our attention. . . . A loving silence often has far more power to heal and to connect than the most well intentioned words.

—RACHEL NAOMI REMEN

Loving and Being Loved

WHEN WE SAY "LOVE," THE FIRST THING THAT POPS INTO our minds is romantic love, the love for a spouse or a partner, or the first person we ever kissed. There is nothing quite so stirring—and disturbing—as the trembling of a new love.

But the enduring loves in our lives may have nothing to do with romance. We love our children, our families, our friends. Loving other people can bring out the best in us. If we're lucky enough to have love in our lives, we sometimes take it for granted. Anyone who has lost someone they love knows just what a mistake that is.

Let yourself love others, and treasure that love. Tell those you love just how much you appreciate having them in your life—and tell them often.

The best thing to hold onto in life is each other.

—AUDREY HEPBURN

Spread love everywhere you go. Let no one ever come to you without leaving happier.

—MOTHER TERESA

The one thing we can never get enough of is love. And the one thing we never give enough of is love.

—HENRY MILLER

Where there is love there is life.

—MAHATMA GANDHI

I love that feeling of being in love, the effect of having butterflies when you wake up in the morning. That is special.

—JENNIFER ANISTON

Love is the greatest refreshment in life.

—Pablo Picasso

To love and be loved is to feel the sun from both sides.

—David Viscott

We waste time looking for the perfect lover, instead of creating the perfect love.

—Tom Robbins

Time is
Too slow for those who wait,
Too swift for those who fear,
Too long for those who grieve,
Too short for those who rejoice;
But for those who love,
Time is eternity.

—Henry Van Dyke

The way to love anything is to realize that it may be lost.

—G.K. Chesterton

Love is an emotion experienced by the many and enjoyed by the few.

—George Jean Nathan

'Tis better to have loved and lost
    than never to have loved at all.

—Alfred, Lord Tennyson

You will find as you look back upon your life that the moments when you have truly lived are the moments when you have done things in the spirit of love.

—Henry Drummond

When you are missing someone, time seems to move slower, and when I'm falling in love with someone, time seems to be moving faster.

—Taylor Swift

Choose your love, love your choice.

—Thomas S. Monson

Love is energy of life.

—ROBERT BROWNING

In our life there is a single color, as on an artist's palette, which provides the meaning of life and art. It is the color of love.

—MARC CHAGALL

The first magic of love is our ignorance that it can ever end.

—BENJAMIN DISRAELI

In life, you have to take the pace that love goes. You don't force it. You just don't force love, you don't force falling in love, you don't force being in love . . . you just feel it.

—JUAN PABLO GALAVIS

Love isn't something you find. Love is something that finds you.

—LORETTA YOUNG

Love does not appear with any warning signs. You fall into it as if pushed from a high diving board. No time to think about what's happening. It's inevitable. An event you can't control. A crazy, heart-stopping, roller-coaster ride that just has to take its course.

—JACKIE COLLINS

Everything is clearer when you're in love.

—JOHN LENNON

~

Get on with living and loving. You don't have forever.

—LEO BUSCAGLIA

~

I am happier when I love than when I am loved. I adore my husband, my son, my grandchildren, my mother, my dog, and frankly, I don't know if they even like me. But who cares? Loving them is my joy.

—ISABEL ALLENDE

~

Loving others always costs us something and requires effort. And you have to decide to do it on purpose. You can't wait for a feeling to motivate you.

—JOYCE MEYER

~

I like being in love, but loving is what is crucial to me. Loving is the reason to live.

—SAFFRON BURROWS

You can't stop loving or wanting to love because when it's right, it's the best thing in the world. When you're in a relationship and it's good, even if nothing else in your life is right, you feel like your whole world is complete.

—KEITH SWEAT

You know you're in love when you can't fall asleep because reality is finally better than your dreams.

—THEODOR GEISEL (A.K.A. DR. SEUSS)

Love recognizes no barriers. It jumps hurdles, leaps fences, penetrates walls to arrive at its destination full of hope.

—MAYA ANGELOU

Being deeply loved by someone gives you strength, while loving someone deeply gives you courage.

—LAO TZU

There is no remedy for love but to love more.

—HENRY DAVID THOREAU

Every heart sings a song, incomplete, until another heart whispers back. Those who wish to sing always find a song. At the touch of a lover, everyone becomes a poet.

—PLATO

Love doesn't just sit there, like a stone, it has to be made, like bread; remade all the time, made new.

—URSULA K. LE GUIN

Romance is the glamour which turns the dust of everyday life into a golden haze.

—ELINOR GLYN

Get to Work

WE MAY GROAN WHEN IT'S TIME TO GET TO WORK, BUT MOST of us realize just how fortunate we are to have something to do each day. If we're very, very lucky, we are able to do work that we love or that makes a difference to others or that challenges us and helps us grow. Or maybe work that compensates us well enough to have a home and take part in activities we enjoy.

We all work, even those of us who don't go to an office and don't collect a paycheck. It may be work we choose, like tending a garden, or it may simply be the tasks we all do to take care of ourselves.

Even the hardest, most unpleasant work has its good moments. The challenge is to recognize and appreciate them—and to understand just how important work is to what we want in life.

Choose a job you love and you will never have to work a day in your life.

—Confucius

~

Nothing ever comes to one, that is worth having, except as a result of hard work.

—Booker T. Washington

~

Opportunity is missed by most people because it is dressed in overalls and looks like work.

—Thomas A. Edison

~

If you're happy in what you're doing, you'll like yourself, you'll have inner peace. And if you have that, along with physical health, you will have had more success than you could possibly have imagined.

—Johnny Carson

~

The best preparation for good work tomorrow is to do good work today.

—Elbert Hubbard

Far and away the best prize that life has to offer is the chance to work hard at work worth doing.

—THEODORE ROOSEVELT

The beginning is the most important part of the work.

—PLATO

I put my heart and my soul into my work, and have lost my mind in the process.

—VINCENT VAN GOGH

Everyone has been made for some particular work, and the desire for that work has been put in every heart.

—RUMI

To fulfill a dream, to be allowed to sweat over lonely labor, to be given a chance to create, is the meat and potatoes of life. The money is the gravy.

—BETTE DAVIS

The supreme accomplishment is to blur the line between work and play.

—Arnold J. Toynbee

~

Laziness may appear attractive, but work gives satisfaction.

—Anne Frank

~

Every man loves what he is good at.

—Thomas Shadwell

~

I approach each project with a new insecurity, almost like the first project I ever did. And I get the sweats. I go in and start working, I'm not sure where I'm going. If I knew where I was going I wouldn't do it.

—Frank Gehry

~

When your work speaks for itself, don't interrupt.

—Henry J. Kaiser

There comes a time when you ought to start doing what you want. Take a job that you love. You will jump out of bed in the morning. I think you are out of your mind if you keep taking jobs that you don't like because you think it will look good on your résumé. Isn't that a little like saving up sex for your old age?

—WARREN BUFFETT

What you are will show in what you do.

—Thomas A. Edison

My experience has been that work is almost the best way
to pull oneself out of the depths.

—Eleanor Roosevelt

To find joy in work is to discover the fountain of youth.

—Pearl S. Buck

There is joy in work. There is no happiness except in the
realization that we have accomplished something.

—Henry Ford

Every man's work, whether it be literature, or music
or pictures or architecture or anything else, is always
a portrait of himself.

—Samuel Butler

It is your work in life that is the ultimate seduction.

—Pablo Picasso

~

I think about my work every minute of the day.

—Jeff Koons

~

Work is not man's punishment. It is his reward and his strength and his pleasure.

—George Sand

~

Work is much more fun than fun.

—Noël Coward

~

The more I want to get something done, the less I call it work.

—Richard Bach

~

Work isn't to make money; you work to justify life.

—Marc Chagall

If it falls your lot to be a street sweeper, go out and sweep streets like Michelangelo painted pictures. Sweep streets like Handel and Beethoven composed music. Sweep streets like Shakespeare wrote poetry. Sweep streets so well that all the hosts of heaven and earth will have to pause and say, "Here lived a great street sweeper who swept his job well."

—Martin Luther King, Jr.

I have found in work that you only get back what you put into it, but it does come back gift-wrapped.

—JOYCE BROTHERS

It is only when I am doing my work that I feel truly alive.

—FEDERICO FELLINI

Don't be afraid to give your best to what seemingly are small jobs. Every time you conquer one it makes you that much stronger. If you do the little jobs well, the big ones will tend to take care of themselves.

—DALE CARNEGIE

Your work is going to fill a large part of your life, and the only way to be truly satisfied is to do what you believe is great work. And the only way to do great work is to love what you do.

—STEVE JOBS

You are not your résumé, you are your work.

—SETH GODIN

I have looked in the mirror every morning and asked myself: "If today were the last day of my life, would I want to do what I am about to do today?" And whenever the answer has been "No" for too many days in a row, I know I need to change something.

—STEVE JOBS

Richer and Poorer

IF WE HAVE ENOUGH MONEY TO TAKE CARE OF OUR BASIC NEEDS and wants—no matter what "basic" means to each of us—we should consider ourselves lucky. But there is a human instinct to want more. Just a little bit would make us more comfortable, wouldn't it?

Seizing the day in terms of wealth doesn't mean spending what we have just to feel good at the moment; it simply means appreciating how the resources we have enhance our lives—and understanding that greater resources won't necessarily do more for us.

Budget your resources—money, certainly, but also time—in ways that bring joy into your life.

If we command our wealth, we shall be rich and free; if our wealth commands us, we are poor indeed.

—Edmund Burke

He is richest who is content with the least, for content is the wealth of nature.

—Socrates

Wealth is the ability to fully experience life.

—Henry David Thoreau

Wealth consists not in having great possessions, but in having few wants.

—Epictetus

When I was young I thought that money was the most important thing in life; now that I am old I know that it is.

—Oscar Wilde

A wise man should have money in his head, but not in his heart.

—JONATHAN SWIFT

Don't let making a living prevent you from making a life.

—JOHN WOODEN

If you make a living, if you earn your own money, you're free—however free one can be on this planet.

—THEODORE WHITE

Money is only a tool. It will take you wherever you wish, but it will not replace you as the driver.

—AYN RAND

It's a kind of spiritual snobbery that makes people think they can be happy without money.

—ALBERT CAMUS

Money is better than poverty, if only for financial reasons.

—Woody Allen

Money can't buy love, but it improves your bargaining position.

—Christopher Marlowe

Too many people spend money they haven't earned to buy things they don't want to impress people they don't like.

—Will Rogers

I'd like to live as a poor man with lots of money.

—Pablo Picasso

The importance of money flows from it being a link between the present and the future.

—John Maynard Keynes

I have no money, no resources, no hopes. I am the happiest man alive.

—HENRY MILLER

If saving money is wrong, I don't want to be right.

—WILLIAM SHATNER

Money does not make you happy but it quiets the nerves.

—SEAN O'CASEY

Liking money like I like it, is nothing less than mysticism. Money is a glory.

—SALVADOR DALÍ

Sudden money is going from zero to two hundred dollars a week. The rest doesn't count.

—NEIL SIMON

There are a handful of people whom money won't spoil, and we all count ourselves among them.

—MIGNON MCLAUGHLIN

~

What's money? A man is a success if he gets up in the morning and goes to bed at night and in between does what he wants to do.

—BOB DYLAN

Learning Over a Lifetime

OUR EDUCATION DOESN'T STOP WHEN WE FINISH SCHOOL. Every day brings the opportunity for new learning, whether it's tackling a task at work that we've never done before, trying a new hobby, or having a spirited discussion with a friend.

One of life's great joys is discovering something new—in other words, learning. That can happen in a classroom or in the middle of an otherwise ordinary day. We enhance our lives when we recognize and welcome those moments.

You are always learning. Accept the lessons each day brings and appreciate how they enhance your life.

In some parts of the world, students are going to school every day. It's their normal life. But in other parts of the world, we are starving for education . . . it's like a precious gift. It's like a diamond.

—Malala Yousafzai

Education is not preparation for life; education is life itself.

—John Dewey

Education is the key to unlock the golden door of freedom.

—George Washington Carver

The whole purpose of education is to turn mirrors into windows.

—Sydney J. Harris

Education is not the filling of a pail, but the lighting of a fire.

—William Butler Yeats

You are always a student, never a master. You have to keep moving forward.

—CONRAD HALL

Education is learning what you didn't even know you didn't know.

—DANIEL J. BOORSTIN

Man is what he reads.

—JOSEPH BRODSKY

The object of education is to prepare the young to educate themselves throughout their lives.

—ROBERT M. HUTCHINS

Education's purpose is to replace an empty mind with an open one.

—MALCOLM FORBES

What sculpture is to a block of marble, education is to the soul.

—JOSEPH ADDISON

He that loves reading has everything within his reach.

—WILLIAM GODWIN

The simplest schoolboy is now familiar with truths for which Archimedes would have sacrificed his life.

—ERNEST RENAN

Your library is your paradise.

—DESIDERIUS ERASMUS

A human being is not attaining his full heights until he is educated.

—HORACE MANN

He who laughs most, learns best.

—JOHN CLEESE

Nine-tenths of education is encouragement.

—ANATOLE FRANCE

I am a part of everything that I have read.

—THEODORE ROOSEVELT

Education is the transmission of civilization.

—WILL DURANT

Education is hanging around until you've caught on.

—ROBERT FROST

It is what you read when you don't have to that determines what you will be when you can't help it.

—OSCAR WILDE

Try to learn something about everything and everything about something.

—THOMAS HUXLEY

~

I kept always two books in my pocket, one to read, one to write in.

—ROBERT LOUIS STEVENSON

~

You can never get a cup of tea large enough or a book long enough to suit me.

—C.S. LEWIS

~

Live as if you were to die tomorrow. Learn as if you were to live forever.

—MAHATMA GANDHI

~

There is no end to education. It is not that you read a book, pass an examination, and finish with education. The whole of life, from the moment you are born to the moment you die, is a process of learning.

—JIDDU KRISHNAMURTI

I am always doing that which I cannot do, in order that
I may learn how to do it.

—PABLO PICASSO

A wise man can learn more from a foolish question than a
fool can learn from a wise answer.

—BRUCE LEE

It's what you learn after you know it all that counts.

—JOHN WOODEN

You cannot open a book without learning something.

—CONFUCIUS

I am always ready to learn, although I do not always like
being taught.

—WINSTON CHURCHILL

Question everything. Learn something. Answer nothing.

—Euripides

I never learn anything talking. I only learn things when I ask questions.

—Lou Holtz

The noblest pleasure is the joy of understanding.

—Leonardo da Vinci

I don't love studying. I hate studying. I like learning. Learning is beautiful.

—Natalie Portman

I'd rather learn from one bird how to sing
    than teach ten thousand stars how not to dance

—E.E. cummings

It's not the teaching, it's the learning.

—Sly Stone

I have never met a man so ignorant that I couldn't learn something from him.

—Galileo Galilei

The minute that you're not learning, I believe you're dead.

—Jack Nicholson

I grow old learning something new every day.

—Solon

Don't Worry, Be Happy

WE CAN'T REALLY PLAN FOR HAPPINESS, AND WE USUALLY can't make it last. What we can do, of course, is enjoy every bit of it to the fullest. If we start worrying about whether or not we deserve to be happy, or whether this feeling will fade (of course it will), we lose the chance to just . . . be happy.

We should be open to happiness, which sometimes seems to sneak up on us. A good meal, the smell of a flower, the sound of birds or crickets or someone we love . . . so many small moments can make us smile, if we simply stop to notice and enjoy them.

Choose to be happy.

I am determined to be cheerful and happy in whatever situation I may find myself. For I have learned that the greater part of our misery or unhappiness is determined not by our circumstance but by our disposition.

—MARTHA WASHINGTON

The best way to pay for a lovely moment is to enjoy it.

—RICHARD BACH

Happiness often sneaks in through a door you didn't know you left open.

—JOHN BARRYMORE

Everything has its wonders, even darkness and silence, and I learn, whatever state I may be in, therein to be content.

—HELEN KELLER

Most folks are as happy as they make up their minds to be.

—ABRAHAM LINCOLN

The moments of happiness we enjoy take us by surprise.
It is not that we seize them, but that they seize us.

—ASHLEY MONTAGU

If you want to be happy, be.

—LEO TOLSTOY

Happiness is like a kiss. You must share to enjoy it.

—BERNARD MELTZER

The Constitution only gives people the right to pursue
happiness. You have to catch it yourself.

—BENJAMIN FRANKLIN

We are no longer happy so soon as we wish to be
happier.

—WALTER SAVAGE LANDOR

Every morning, when we wake up, we have twenty-four brand-new hours to live. What a precious gift! We have the capacity to live in a way that these twenty-four hours will bring peace, joy, and happiness to ourselves and others.

—Thich Nhat Hanh

I, not events, have the power to make me happy or unhappy
today. I can choose which it shall be. Yesterday is dead,
tomorrow hasn't arrived yet. I have just one day, today,
and I'm going to be happy in it.

—GROUCHO MARX

Don't wait around for other people to be happy for you.
Any happiness you get you've got to make yourself.

—ALICE WALKER

I caught the happiness virus last night
    When I was out singing beneath the stars.

—HAFIZ OF PERSIA

My life has no purpose, no direction, no aim, no meaning, and
yet I'm happy. I can't figure it out. What am I doing right?

—CHARLES M. SCHULZ

The foolish man seeks happiness in the distance; the wise
grows it under his feet.

—JAMES OPPENHEIM

Those who bring sunshine into the lives of others cannot keep it from themselves.

—James M. Barrie

The pursuit of happiness is a most ridiculous phrase; if you pursue happiness, you'll never find it.

—C.P. Snow

Do not look back on happiness or dream of it in the future. You are only sure of today; do not let yourself be cheated out of it.

—Henry Ward Beecher

I arise in the morning torn between a desire to improve (or save) the world and a desire to enjoy (or savor) the world. This makes it hard to plan the day.

—E.B. White

Moderation. Small helpings. Sample a little bit of everything. These are the secrets of happiness and good health.

—Julia Child

Don't waste a minute not being happy. If one window
closes, run to the next window—or break down a door.

—BROOKE SHIELDS

Man is fond of counting his troubles, but he does not count
his joys. If he counted them up as he ought to, he would see
that every lot has enough happiness provided for it.

—FYODOR DOSTOEVSKY

If only we'd stop trying to be happy, we could have a pretty
good time.

—EDITH WHARTON

Happiness is like a butterfly which, when pursued, is
always beyond our grasp, but, if you will sit down quietly,
may alight upon you.

—NATHANIEL HAWTHORNE

One joy scatters a hundred griefs.

—CHINESE PROVERB

Learn to let go. That is the key to happiness.

—BUDDHA

For every minute you are angry, you lose sixty seconds of happiness.

—RALPH WALDO EMERSON

There are some days when I think I'm going to die from an overdose of satisfaction.

—SALVADOR DALÍ

It's a helluva start, being able to recognize what makes you happy.

—LUCILLE BALL

A table, a chair, a bowl of fruit and a violin; what else does a man need to be happy?

—ALBERT EINSTEIN

Now and then it's good to pause in our pursuit of happiness and just be happy.

—GUILLAUME APOLLINAIRE

~

Happy he who learns to bear what he cannot change.

—FRIEDRICH SCHILLER

When Life Gets Tough

HOW DO WE SEIZE THE DAY WHEN THE DAY IS LOUSY? OUR ability to enjoy the moment is tested when the moment is something we want to get through as quickly as possible.

Seizing the moment becomes even more important when we're in the middle of crisis or feel consumed by problems. We can focus on the positive—even when we're overwhelmed, we can savor a good cup of coffee, or enjoy a laugh with a friend. But we can also look at the problems or challenges in front of us and understand that dealing with them may make us stronger, better, and even happier in the long run.

Remember that bad times don't have to last, and that there is joy even in the most difficult situations.

The only use of an obstacle is to be overcome. All that an obstacle does with brave men is, not to frighten them, but to challenge them.

—WOODROW WILSON

The most glorious moments in your life are not the so-called days of success, but rather those days when out of dejection and despair, you feel rise in you a challenge to life, and the promise of future accomplishments.

—GUSTAVE FLAUBERT

I think men, growing up, you have to go through some form of hardship. You've got to harden the metal.

—ICE-T

There are uses to adversity, and they don't reveal themselves until tested. Whether it's serious illness, financial hardship, or the simple constraint of parents who speak limited English, difficulty can tap unexpected strengths.

—SONIA SOTOMAYOR

Sorrow happens, hardship happens.
    The hell with it. Who never knew
the price of happiness will not be happy.

—YEVGENY YEVTUSHENKO

The moments that make life worth living are when things
are at their worst and you find a way to laugh.

—AMY SCHUMER

The greater the obstacle, the more glory in overcoming it.

—MOLIÈRE

I have not failed. I've just found 10,000 ways that won't work.

—THOMAS A. EDISON

Some luck lies in not getting what you thought you
wanted but getting what you have, which once you
have got it you may be smart enough to see is what
you would have wanted had you known.

—GARRISON KEILLOR

It just wouldn't be a picnic without the ants.

—AUTHOR UNKNOWN

The problem is not that there are problems. The problem is expecting otherwise and thinking that having problems is a problem.

—THEODORE RUBIN

I have sometimes been wildly, despairingly, acutely miserable, but through it all I still know quite certainly that just to be alive is a grand thing.

—AGATHA CHRISTIE

When you come out of the storm, you won't be the same person who walked in. That's what this storm's all about.

—HARUKI MURAKAMI

Smooth seas do not make skillful sailors.

—AFRICAN PROVERB

Even our misfortunes are part of our belongings.

—Antoine de Saint-Exupéry

Every problem has in it the seeds of its own solution. If you don't have any problems, you don't get any seeds.

—Norman Vincent Peale

A problem is a chance for you to do your best.

—Duke Ellington

Don't cry when the sun is gone, because the tears won't let you see the stars.

—Violeta Parra

One who fears the future, who fears failure, limits his activities. Failure is only the opportunity to more intelligently begin again.

—Henry Ford

I've missed more than 9,000 shots in my career. I've lost almost 300 games. Twenty-six times, I've been trusted to take the game-winning shot and missed. I've failed over and over and over again in my life. And that is why I succeed.

—MICHAEL JORDAN

Failure is the condiment that gives success its flavor.

—TRUMAN CAPOTE

Problems are messages.

—SHAKTI GAWAIN

Failure happens all the time. It happens every day in practice. What makes you better is how you react to it.

—MIA HAMM

Success isn't permanent and failure isn't fatal.

—MIKE DITKA

Every strike brings me closer to the next home run.

—BABE RUTH

A life spent making mistakes is not only more honorable, but more useful than a life spent doing nothing.

—GEORGE BERNARD SHAW

In Sickness and in Health

THERE'S NOTHING LIKE BEING ILL—OR SEEING SOMEONE ELSE COPE with illness—to make us appreciate what we have. After a few weeks on crutches, we treasure the ability to walk unassisted. A bout with intestinal flu makes us happy just to be free of aches and chills, once we're on the way to recovery. We tend to take our good health for granted until we lose it or risk losing it.

But even without the blessing of good health, many people find ways to treasure and enjoy what they have. Recent research has shown that those we might expect to be depressed or unhappy because they have lost limbs or sight or other abilities are often better at finding joy in their lives than those who don't face that kind of health challenge.

When you're in good health, take a moment to think about just how much pleasure that brings to every day. And when you are ill, or your body isn't as strong as it once was, still savor every activity and every moment you can.

I have been very blessed in my life and rewarded with good friends and good health. I am grateful and happy to be able to share this.

—ERIC IDLE

You don't have to be a wreck. You don't have to be sick. One's aim in life should be to die in good health. Just like a candle that burns out.

—JEANNE MOREAU

Good health and good sense are two of life's greatest blessings.

—PUBLILIUS SYRUS

Happiness is good health and a bad memory.

—INGRID BERGMAN

I am confident that nobody . . . will accuse me of selfishness if I ask to spend time, while I am still in good health, with my family, my friends, and also with myself.

—NELSON MANDELA

If we are creating ourselves all the time, then it is never too late to begin creating the bodies we want instead of the ones we mistakenly assume we are stuck with.

—DEEPAK CHOPRA

I reckon being ill as one of the great pleasures of life, provided one is not too ill and is not obliged to work till one is better.

—SAMUEL BUTLER

To feel keenly the poetry of a morning's roses, one has to have just escaped from the claws of this vulture which we call sickness.

—HENRI-FRÉDÉRIC AMIEL

A good laugh and a long sleep are the best cures in the doctor's book.

—IRISH PROVERB

He who can believe himself well, will be well.

—OVID

If one's bowels move, one is happy; and if they don't move, one is unhappy. That is all there is to it.

—Lin Yutang

From the bitterness of disease man learns the sweetness of health.

—Catalan proverb

I am pretty sure that, if you will be quite honest, you will admit that a good rousing sneeze, one that tears open your collar and throws your hair into your eyes, is really one of life's sensational pleasures.

—Robert Benchley

It is part of the cure to wish to be cured.

—Seneca

Health is the first muse, comprising the magical benefits of air, landscape, and bodily exercise on the mind.

—Ralph Waldo Emerson

I am convinced that unconditional love is the most powerful known stimulant of the immune system. If I told patients to raise their blood levels of immune globulins or killer T cells, no one would know how. But if I can teach them to love themselves and others fully, the same changes happen automatically. The truth is: love heals.

—BERNIE SIEGEL

Illness tells us what we are.

—Italian saying

He who has health has hope; and he who has hope
has everything.

—Arabic proverb

To keep the body in good health is a duty, otherwise we
shall not be able to keep our mind strong and clear.

—Buddha

The secret of health for both mind and body is not to
mourn for the past, not to worry about the future, or
not to anticipate troubles, but to live the present moment
wisely and earnestly.

—Buddha

Use your health, even to the point of wearing it out. That
is what it is for. Spend all you have before you die; and do
not outlive yourself.

—George Bernard Shaw

Sedentary people are apt to have sluggish minds. A sluggish mind is apt to be reflected in flabbiness of body and in a dullness of expression that invites no interest and gets none.

—Rose Kennedy

A vigorous five-mile walk will do more good for an unhappy but otherwise healthy adult than all the medicine and psychology in the world.

—Paul Dudley White

To me, good health is more than just exercise and diet. It's really a point of view and a mental attitude you have about yourself.

—Albert Schweitzer

Walking is the best possible exercise. Habituate yourself to walk very far.

—Thomas Jefferson

The Art of Living

IT'S A RARE PERSON WHO DOESN'T INTERACT WITH ART ON A DAILY basis. We turn on the radio while we're driving, or we see framed paintings or posters when we go into the bank. We might see a mime trying to make a living on a busy street corner. And we watch television and read a popular novel.

High art, low art . . . it's everywhere. It enriches our lives, even when we don't pay attention to it. If we pay attention, even when the moment goes by quickly, we are able to interact with art more profoundly.

Get the most out of the art you encounter. Stop, even for just a few seconds, to wonder at and enjoy the art you see, hear, watch, read, or feel.

Art is the only way to run away without leaving home.

—Twyla Tharp

Life beats down and crushes the soul and art reminds you that you have one.

—Stella Adler

Art is the stored honey of the human soul, gathered on wings of misery and travail.

—Theodore Dreiser

I think music in itself is healing. It's an explosive expression of humanity. It's something we are all touched by. No matter what culture we're from, everyone loves music.

—Billy Joel

Great art picks up where nature ends.

—Marc Chagall

What art offers is space—a certain breathing room for the spirit.

—JOHN UPDIKE

Great art is as irrational as great music. It is mad with its own loveliness.

—GEORGE JEAN NATHAN

And who hears music feels his solitude
   Peopled at once.

—ROBERT BROWNING

Every child is an artist until he's told he's not an artist.

—JOHN LENNON

As the sun colors flowers, so does art color life.

—JOHN LUBBOCK

Art is like a border of flowers along the course of civilization.

—Lincoln Steffens

~

Music in the soul can be heard by the universe.

—Lao Tzu

~

Music can change the world because it can change people.

—Bono

~

Music washes away from the soul the dust of everyday life.

—Berthold Auerbach

~

Without music, life would be a mistake.

—Friedrich Nietzsche

~

You are the music
    While the music lasts

—T.S. Eliot

Music is the soundtrack of your life.

—DICK CLARK

Music is the best means we have of digesting time.

—IGOR STRAVINSKY

Dance is the hidden language of the soul of the body.

—MARTHA GRAHAM

The dance is a poem of which each movement is a word.

—MATA HARI

To dance is to be out of yourself. Larger, more beautiful, more powerful. This is power, it is glory on earth and it is yours for the taking.

—AGNES DE MILLE

Poetry is what in a poem makes you laugh, cry, prickle, be silent, makes your toe nails twinkle, makes you want to do this or that or nothing, makes you know that you are alone in the unknown world, that your bliss and suffering is forever shared and forever all your own.

—Dylan Thomas

I found that dance, music, and literature is how I made sense of the world . . . it pushed me to think of things bigger than life's daily routines . . . to think beyond what is immediate or convenient.

—MIKHAIL BARYSHNIKOV

The one thing that you have that nobody else has is you. Your voice, your mind, your story, your vision. So write and draw and build and play and dance and live as only you can.

—NEIL GAIMAN

Those move easiest who have learn'd to dance.

—ALEXANDER POPE

Poetry is language at its most distilled and most powerful.

—RITA DOVE

There is not a particle of life which does not bear poetry within it.

—GUSTAVE FLAUBERT

Genuine poetry can communicate before it is understood.

—T.S. Eliot

Poetry is an echo asking a shadow dancer to be a partner.

—Carl Sandburg

I regard the theater as the greatest of all art forms, the most immediate way in which a human being can share with another the sense of what it is to be a human being.

—Oscar Wilde

Cinema should make you forget you are sitting in a theater.

—Roman Polanski

Everybody has something that chews them up and, for me, that thing was always loneliness. The cinema has the power to make you not feel lonely, even when you are.

—Tom Hanks

Literature adds to reality. It does not simply describe it. It enriches the necessary competencies that daily life requires and provides; and in this respect, it irrigates the deserts that our lives have already become.

—C.S. Lewis

No matter what is happening in life or in the world— war, natural disaster, poor health, pain, the death of loved ones—if existence is filled with art, music, and literature, life will be fulfilling, a joy.

—Karen DeCrow

The answers you get from literature depend on the questions you pose.

—Margaret Atwood

Literature is one of the most interesting and significant expressions of humanity.

—P.T. Barnum

Literature is a luxury; fiction is a necessity.

—G.K. CHESTERTON

The only substitute for an experience which we have not ourselves lived through is art and literature.

—ALEKSANDR SOLZHENITSYN

Literature and butterflies are the two sweetest passions known to man.

—VLADIMIR NABOKOV

If you can't be a poet, be the poem.

—DAVID CARRADINE

Back to Nature

IN OUR DAILY RUSH, WE MAY NOT TAKE ENOUGH TIME TO APPRECIATE the joys of nature that are all around us. Those of us who live in areas with open vistas or mountains or rivers and lakes may take it all for granted while managing work, family, and personal obligations. No need to notice the bright pink sunrise this morning; there will be another one tomorrow. But how much it enhances our day if we stop to appreciate that sunrise right now.

Those of us who live in more urban places may not have open water or fields, but we still have sunshine and rain, birds, parks, trees, and more. A few minutes sitting on a bench and enjoying the sights, sounds, and touch of nature around us can give us a happier outlook.

Take time to smell the roses, feed the pigeons, lie on the grass. You're a part of nature—and it's an important part of you.

Look deep into nature, and then you will understand everything better.

—ALBERT EINSTEIN

On earth there is no heaven, but there are pieces of it.

—JULES RENARD

Just living is not enough . . . one must have sunshine, freedom, and a little flower.

—HANS CHRISTIAN ANDERSEN

Let the rain kiss you
Let the rain beat upon your head with silver liquid drops
Let the rain sing you a lullaby

—LANGSTON HUGHES

Nature always wears the colors of the spirit.

—RALPH WALDO EMERSON

For after all, the best thing one can do
　When it is raining is to let it rain.

—HENRY WADSWORTH LONGFELLOW

Nature will bear the closest inspection. She invites us to
lay our eye level with the smallest leaf, and take an insect
view of its plain.

—HENRY DAVID THOREAU

The clearest way into the Universe is through a forest
wilderness.

—JOHN MUIR

Sunshine is delicious, rain is refreshing, wind braces us up,
snow is exhilarating; there is really no such thing as bad
weather, only different kinds of good weather.

—JOHN RUSKIN

Forget not that the earth delights to feel your bare feet
and the winds long to play with your hair.

—KHALIL GIBRAN

For my part, I know nothing with any certainty, but the sight of the stars makes me dream.

—Vincent van Gogh

〜

The mountains are calling and I must go.

—John Muir

〜

There are always flowers for those who want to see them.

—Henri Matisse

〜

I go to nature to be soothed and healed, and to have my senses put in order.

—John Burroughs

〜

It is not light that is needed, but fire; it is not the gentle shower, but thunder. We need the storm, the whirlwind, and the earthquake.

—Frederick Douglass

Earth laughs in flowers.

—Ralph Waldo Emerson

In all things of nature there is something of the marvelous.

—Aristotle

It is not so much for its beauty that the forest makes a claim upon men's hearts, as for that subtle something, that quality of air, that emanation from old trees, that so wonderfully changes and renews a weary spirit.

—Robert Louis Stevenson

The sun, with all those planets revolving around it and dependent on it, can still ripen a bunch of grapes as if it had nothing else in the universe to do.

—Galileo Galilei

To sit in the shade on a fine day, and look upon verdure, is the most perfect refreshment.

—Jane Austen

One touch of nature makes the whole world kin.

—WILLIAM SHAKESPEARE

⁓

I remember a hundred lovely lakes, and recall the fragrant breath of pine and fir and cedar and poplar trees. The trail has strung upon it, as upon a thread of silk, opalescent dawns and saffron sunsets.

—HAMLIN GARLAND

⁓

Give me odorous at sunrise a garden of beautiful flowers where I can walk undisturbed.

—WALT WHITMAN

⁓

If people sat outside and looked at the stars each night, I bet they'd live a lot differently.

—BILL WATTERSON

⁓

What is the good of your stars and trees, your sunrise and the wind, if they do not enter into our daily lives?

—E.M. FORSTER

The poetry of the earth is never dead.

—JOHN KEATS

～

Nature, like man, sometimes weeps from gladness.

—BENJAMIN DISRAELI

～

People from a planet without flowers would think we
must be mad with joy the whole time to have such things
about us.

—IRIS MURDOCH

～

When you have seen one ant, one bird, one tree, you have
not seen them all.

—E. O. WILSON

～

The ground we walk on, the plants and creatures, the
clouds above constantly dissolving into new formations—
each gift of nature possessing its own radiant energy,
bound together by cosmic harmony.

—RUTH BERNHARD

Birds sing after a storm; why shouldn't people feel as free to delight in whatever sunlight remains to them?

—Rose Kennedy

I still get wildly enthusiastic about little things . . . I play with leaves. I skip down the street and run against the wind.

—Leo Buscaglia

In wilderness I sense the miracle of life, and behind it our scientific accomplishments fade to trivia.

—Charles Lindbergh

There is the sky, which is all men's together.

—Euripides

When I consider how, after sunset, the stars come out gradually in troops from behind the hills and woods, I confess that I could not have contrived a more curious and inspiring night.

—Henry David Thoreau

To Every Thing, There Is a Season

IF WE LIVE SOMEWHERE WITH DISTINCT AND VERY DIFFERENT seasons—broiling summer suns and frigid winter snows— we may find ourselves wishing for cooler temperatures in July and a melt in January, as if we're never satisfied with the season we're in.

Each season has its own particular and fleeting joys, whether it's seeing the first robin or the last flame-red maple leaf. Even when we live somewhere the seasons change subtly, we can notice and enjoy those changes as they happen.

Live in the season and appreciate the signs that tell us Earth is turning and changing every day.

Every corny thing that's said about living with nature—
being in harmony with the earth, feeling the cycle of the
seasons—happens to be true.

—SUSAN ORLEAN

The spring, summer, is quite a hectic time for people in
their lives, but then it comes to autumn, and to winter, and
you can't but help think back to the year that was, and then
hopefully looking forward to the year that is approaching.

—ENYA

Spring is nature's way of saying, "Let's party!"

—ROBIN WILLIAMS

Oh, Spring! I want to go out and feel you and get
inspiration. My old things seem dead. I want fresh
contacts, more vital searching.

—EMILY CARR

It will not always be summer; build barns.

—HESIOD

Spring won't let me stay in this house any longer! I must get out and breathe the air deeply again.

—GUSTAV MAHLER

I am going to notice the lights of the earth, the sun and the moon and stars, the lights of our candles as we march, the lights with which spring teases us, the light that is already present.

—ANNE LAMOTT

In the spring, at the end of the day, you should smell like dirt.

—MARGARET ATWOOD

No man can taste the fruits of autumn while he is delighting his scent with the flowers of spring.

—SAMUEL JOHNSON

People don't notice whether it's winter or summer when they're happy.

—ANTON CHEKHOV

It was a splendid summer morning and it seemed as if nothing could go wrong.

—JOHN CHEEVER

Summer afternoon—summer afternoon; to me those have always been the two most beautiful words in the English language.

—HENRY JAMES

Ah, summer, what power you have to make us suffer and like it.

—RUSSELL BAKER

The summer night is like a perfection of thought.

—WALLACE STEVENS

Summer is the time when one sheds one's tensions with one's clothes, and the right kind of day is jeweled balm for the battered spirit. A few of those days and you can become drunk with the belief that all's right with the world.

—ADA LOUISE HUXTABLE

Aaah, summer—that long anticipated stretch of lazy, lingering days, free of responsibility and rife with possibility. It's a time to hunt for insects, master handstands, practice swimming strokes, conquer trees, explore nooks and crannies, and make new friends.

—DARELL HAMMOND

August brings into sharp focus and a furious boil everything
I've been listening to in the late spring and summer.

—HENRY ROLLINS

A woodland in full color is awesome as a forest fire, in
magnitude at least, but a single tree is like a dancing
tongue of flame to warm the heart.

—HAL BORLAND

What good is the warmth of summer, without the cold of
winter to give it sweetness.

—JOHN STEINBECK

. . . there is a harmony
    In autumn, and a luster in its sky,
Which through the summer is not heard or seen,
    As if it could not be, as if it had not been!

—PERCY BYSSHE SHELLEY

Autumn's the mellow time.

—WILLIAM ALLINGHAM

Summer ends, and Autumn comes, and he who would have
it otherwise would have high tide always and a full moon
every night.

—HAL BORLAND

I know the lands are lit
   With all the autumn blaze of Golden Rod

—HELEN HUNT JACKSON

Life starts all over again when it gets crisp in the fall.

—F. SCOTT FITZGERALD

Autumn carries more gold in its pocket than all the
other seasons.

—JIM BISHOP

It is the life of the crystal, the architect of the flake,
the fire of the frost, the soul of the sunbeam. This crisp
winter air is full of it.

—JOHN BURROUGHS

Every leaf speaks bliss to me
Fluttering from the autumn tree.

—EMILY BRONTË

Autumn, the year's last, loveliest smile.

—WILLIAM CULLEN BRYANT

I'm so glad I live in a world where there are Octobers.

—L. M. MONTGOMERY

Winter is a season of recovery and preparation.

—PAUL THEROUX

Even in winter an isolated patch of snow has a special quality.

—ANDY GOLDSWORTHY

You can't get too much winter in the winter.

—ROBERT FROST

I love the scents of winter! For me, it's all about the feeling you get when you smell pumpkin spice, cinnamon, nutmeg, gingerbread, and spruce.

—TAYLOR SWIFT

I prefer winter and fall, when you feel the bone structure of the landscape. . . . Something waits beneath it—the whole story doesn't show.

—ANDREW WYETH

Let us love winter, for it is the spring of genius.

—PIETRO ARETINO

Thank goodness for the first snow, it was a reminder—no matter how old you became and how much you'd seen, things could still be new if you were willing to believe they still mattered.

—CANDACE BUSHNELL

As Old As We Feel

CHILDREN CAN'T WAIT TO GET OLDER; ADULTS SEEM TO HAVE ALL the advantages. Students want to get through school and graduate to "get on with life." We want to find a partner or buy a house or get a promotion. It's all about moving ahead, faster and faster, until . . .

Every age has its good times and bad times, but too often we're too busy looking backward or forward at our lives to just enjoy right where we are. As we get into the "senior" years, we tend to want to squeeze every bit of juice we can out of each day; wouldn't it be great if we could do that at every stage of our lives?

Without getting morbid about it, remind yourself that our days are limited. Even if you live to be 100, that's only 100 summers, 100 New Year's Eves—39,000 days to enjoy. Make each day count, no matter how many or how few you think are ahead of you.

Age is an issue of mind over matter. If you don't mind, it doesn't matter.

—AUTHOR UNKNOWN

The trick is growing up without growing old.

—CASEY STENGEL

He who is of a calm and happy nature will hardly feel the pressure of age, but to him who is of an opposite disposition, youth and age are equally a burden.

—PLATO

Aging is not lost youth but a new stage of opportunity and strength.

—BETTY FRIEDAN

The aging process has you firmly in its grasp if you never get the urge to throw a snowball.

—DOUG LARSON

Aging can be fun if you lay back and enjoy it.

—CLINT EASTWOOD

We don't stop playing because we grow old. We grow old because we stop playing.

—G. STANLEY HALL

The great secret that all old people share is that you really haven't changed in seventy or eighty years. Your body changes, but you don't change at all. And that, of course, causes great confusion.

—DORIS LESSING

Too many people, when they get old, think that they have to live by the calendar.

—JOHN GLENN

Today is the oldest you've ever been, and the youngest you'll ever be again.

—ELEANOR ROOSEVELT

Laughter is timeless. Imagination has no age. And dreams are forever.

—WALT DISNEY

None are so old as those who have outlived enthusiasm.

—HENRY DAVID THOREAU

Anyone who stops learning is old, whether at twenty or eighty. Anyone who keeps learning stays young.

—HENRY FORD

To know how to grow old is the master-work of wisdom, and one of the most difficult chapters in the great art of living.

—HENRI-FRÉDÉRIC AMIEL

Grow old along with me!
    The best is yet to be

—ROBERT BROWNING

The longer I live, the more beautiful life becomes.

—FRANK LLOYD WRIGHT

A man is not old until regrets take the place of dreams.

—JOHN BARRYMORE

Everyone is the age of their heart.

—GUATEMALAN PROVERB

It's sad to grow old, but nice to ripen.

—BRIGITTE BARDOT

To be old can be glorious if one has not unlearned how to begin.

—MARTIN BUBER

A man is not old as long as he is seeking something.

—JEAN ROSTAND

We turn not older with years, but newer every day.

—EMILY DICKINSON

Old age ain't no place for sissies.

—BETTE DAVIS

There are years that ask questions and years that answer.

—ZORA NEALE HURSTON

Growing old is a bad habit which a busy man has no time to form.

—ANDRÉ MAUROIS

It takes a very long time to become young.

—PABLO PICASSO

Old age transfigures or fossilizes.

—MARIE VON EBNER-ESCHENBACH

To keep the heart unwrinkled, to be hopeful, kindly, cheerful, reverent—that is to triumph over old age.

—THOMAS BAILEY ALDRICH

The best way to judge a life is to ask yourself, "Did I make the best use of the time I had?"

—ARTHUR ASHE

As you get older, the questions come down to about two or three. How long? And what do I do with the time I've got left?

—DAVID BOWIE

Good gracious! What there is to admire and how little time there is to see it in! For the first time, one begins to envy Methuselah.

—WINSTON CHURCHILL

Age is just a number. It's totally irrelevant, unless, of course, you happen to be a bottle of wine.

—JOAN COLLINS

As we grow old . . . the beauty steals inward.

—Ralph Waldo Emerson

If you have anything better to be doing when you are so overtaken [by death], get to work on that.

—Epictetus

It's a Wonderful Day

GRABBING THE JOY, THE LOVE, AND THE WONDER OF EACH DAY IS a habit any of us can acquire. There's a sort-of joke some seniors toss around, about being happy just to wake up in the morning. Well, they may have it right.

We can all feel privileged to live each day, to use whatever faculties we have in the best ways possible, to enjoy the company of friends and family, to "indulge" ourselves in a good meal, a favorite piece of music, a scented candle, a long nap.

Every day is a gift, with moments for happiness within it. Notice the positives in your life and enjoy them to the fullest.

When you arise in the morning, think of what a privilege
it is to be alive—to breathe, to think, to enjoy, to love.

—MARCUS AURELIUS

Every day brings a chance for you to draw in a breath,
kick off your shoes, and step out and dance.

—OPRAH WINFREY

Nothing is worth more than this day.

—JOHANN WOLFGANG VON GOETHE

Don't be too timid and squeamish about your actions.
All life is an experiment. The more experiments you
make, the better.

—RALPH WALDO EMERSON

I don't have to be perfect. All I have to do is show up and
enjoy the messy, imperfect, and beautiful journey of my
life. It's a trip more wonderful than I could have imagined.

—KERRY WASHINGTON

How we spend our days is, of course, how we spend our lives.

—ANNIE DILLARD

Let all of life be an unfettered howl.

—VLADIMIR NABOKOV

Live to the point of tears.

—ALBERT CAMUS

Life is either a daring adventure or nothing.

—HELEN KELLER

You live but once; you might as well be amusing.

—COCO CHANEL

Forever—is composed of Nows—

—EMILY DICKINSON

The miracle is not to walk on water. The miracle is to walk on the green earth, dwelling deeply in the present moment and feeling truly alive.

—THICH NHAT HANH

Wake up and live.

—BOB MARLEY

Seize the moment. Remember all those women on the *Titanic* who waved off the dessert cart.

—ERMA BOMBECK

If you walk down the street and smile at someone, that will get passed on to the next person. That has the power to change someone's day.

—JULIANNA MARGULIES

A man who dares to waste one hour of time has not discovered the value of life.

—CHARLES DARWIN

A single day is enough to make us a little larger.

—PAUL KLEE

—

Whether it's the best of times or the worst of times, it's the only time we've got.

—ART BUCHWALD

—

Look at the sparrows; they do not know what they will do in the next moment. Let us literally live from moment to moment.

—GANDHI

—

When it comes to life, the critical thing is whether you take things for granted or take them with gratitude.

—G.K. CHESTERTON

—

How wonderful it is that nobody need wait a single moment before starting to improve the world.

—ANNE FRANK

There comes a time in your life when you have to let go of all the pointless drama and the people who create it, and surround yourself with people who make you laugh so hard that you forget the bad and focus solely on the good. After all, life is too short to be anything but happy.

—KARL MARX

The journey of a thousand miles begins with one step.

—Lao Tzu

~

The aim of life is to live, and to live means to be aware, joyously, drunkenly, serenely, divinely aware.

—Henry Miller

~

Take wrong turns. Talk to strangers. Open unmarked doors. And if you see a group of people in a field, go find out what they are doing. Do things without always knowing how they'll turn out.

—Randall Munroe

~

Life is a great big canvas and you should throw all the paint on it you can.

—Danny Kaye

~

Life is not a problem to be solved, but a reality to be experienced.

—J.J. Van Der Leeuw

You must do the thing you think you cannot do.

—ELEANOR ROOSEVELT

The best time to plant a tree was twenty years ago. The second best time is now.

—CHINESE PROVERB

Life is beautiful, as long as it consumes you. When it is rushing through you, destroying you, life is gorgeous, glorious. It's when you burn a slow fire and save fuel that life's not worth having.

—D.H. LAWRENCE

Keep your head high, keep your chin up, and most importantly, keep smiling, because life's a beautiful thing and there's so much to smile about.

—MARILYN MONROE

Dwell on the beauty of life. Watch the stars and see yourself running with them.

—MARCUS AURELIUS

Be happy for this moment. This moment is your life.

—OMAR KHAYYAM

Life is short, break the rules. Forgive quickly, kiss slowly. Love truly. Laugh uncontrollably and never regret anything that makes you smile.

—MARK TWAIN

I find ecstasy in living; the mere sense of living is joy enough.

—EMILY DICKINSON

Do anything, but let it produce joy.

—WALT WHITMAN

The purpose of life, after all, is to live it, to taste experience to the utmost, to reach out eagerly and without fear for newer and richer experience.

—ELEANOR ROOSEVELT

Yesterday is gone. Tomorrow has not yet come. We have only today. Let us begin.

—MOTHER TERESA

Real generosity towards the future lies in giving all to the present.

—ALBERT CAMUS

I still find each day too short for all the thoughts I want to think, all the walks I want to take, all the books I want to read, and all the friends I want to see.

—JOHN BURROUGHS

Set wide the window. Let me drink the day.

—EDITH WHARTON

Write it on your heart that every day is the best day in the year.

—RALPH WALDO EMERSON

You must live in the present, launch yourself on every
wave, find your eternity in each moment. Fools stand on
their island of opportunities and look toward another
land. There is no other land; there is no other life
but this.

—HENRY DAVID THOREAU

~

Happiness, knowledge, not in another place, but this
place—not for another hour, but this hour.

—WALT WHITMAN

~

Tell me, what is it you plan to do
    with your one wild and precious life?

—MARY OLIVER

~

When one has a great deal to put into it, a day has a
hundred pockets.

—FRIEDRICH NIETZSCHE

Spend the afternoon. You can't take it with you.

—ANNIE DILLARD

May you live all the days of your life.

—JONATHAN SWIFT

Excuse me, while I kiss the sky.

—JIMI HENDRIX

The best way to pay for a lovely moment is to
enjoy it.

—RICHARD BACH

The only people for me are the mad ones, the ones who
are mad to live, mad to talk, mad to be saved, desirous
of everything at the same time, the ones who never yawn
or say a commonplace thing but burn, burn, burn like
fabulous yellow roman candles exploding like spiders
across the stars.

—JACK KEROUAC

Contributors

Douglas Adams *(1952–2001)* — British writer, humorist, and playwright

Joseph Addison *(1672–1719)* — British essayist, poet, and playwright

Stella Adler *(1901–1992)* — American actress and acting teacher

Thomas Bailey Aldrich *(1836–1907)* — American magazine editor and poet

Woody Allen *(b. 1935)* — American actor, writer, director, comedian, and playwright

Isabel Allende *(b. 1942)* — Chilean-American writer

William Allingham *(1824–1889)* — Irish poet, diarist, and editor

Henri-Frédéric Amiel *(1821–1881)* — Swiss philosopher, poet, and critic

Hans Christian Andersen *(1805–1875)* — Danish author

Jennifer Aniston *(b. 1969)* — American actor and producer

Guillaume Apollinaire *(1880–1918)* — French poet, playwright, writer, and art critic

Thomas Aquinas *(c. 1225–1274)* — Italian priest, philosopher, theologian, and jurist

Pietro Aretino *(1492–1556)* — Italian author, playwright, and poet

Aristotle *(384–322 BC)* — Greek philosopher

Arthur Ashe *(1943–1993)* — American tennis player and humanitarian

Margaret Atwood *(b. 1939)* — Canadian poet, novelist, and literary critic

Berthold Auerbach *(1812–1882)* — German poet and author

Marcus Aurelius *(121–180)* — Roman emperor and philosopher

Jane Austen *(1775–1817)* — British novelist

Richard Bach *(b. 1936)* — American author

Russell Baker *(b. 1925)* — American writer

Lucille Ball *(1911–1989)* — American actress, film studio executive, and television producer

Brigitte Bardot *(b. 1934)* — French actress, model, animal-rights activist

P.T. Barnum *(1810–1891)* — American showman and businessman

James M. Barrie *(1860–1937)* — Scottish author and dramatist

Ethel Barrymore *(1879–1959)* — American actress

John Barrymore *(1882–1942)* — American actor

Mikhail Baryshnikov (*b. 1948*) — Russian-born American dancer, choreographer, and actor

Henry Ward Beecher *(1813–1887)* — American clergyman and abolitionist

Robert Benchley *(1889–1945)* — American writer, critic, and actor

Elizabeth Berg *(b. 1948)* — American author

Ingrid Bergman *(1915–1982)* — Swedish actress

Ruth Bernhard *(1905–2006)* — German-born American photographer

John Betjeman *(1906–1984)* — British poet, writer, and broadcaster

Jim Bishop *(1907–1987)* — American journalist and author

Erma Bombeck *(1927–1996)* — American humorist and writer

Bono *(b. 1960)* — Irish musician, singer-songwriter, and philanthropist

Daniel J. Boorstin *(1914–2004)* — American historian and twelfth Librarian of Congress

Hal Borland *(1900–1978)* — American author and journalist

David Bowie *(1947–2016)* — British singer, songwriter, record producer, painter, and actor

Ray Bradbury *(1920–2012)* — American writer

Joseph Brodsky *(1940–1996)* — Russian-born American poet and essayist

Emily Brontë *(1818–1848)* — English novelist and poet

Joyce Brothers *(1927–2013)* — American psychologist, writer, and advice columnist

Robert Browning *(1812–1889)* — English poet and playwright

William Cullen Bryant *(1794–1878)* — American poet, journalist, and editor

Martin Buber *(1878–1965)* — Austrian-born Israeli philosopher

Art Buchwald *(1925–2007)* — American writer

Pearl S. Buck *(1892–1973)* — American writer

Gail Lumet Buckley *(b. 1937)* — American writer

Buddha *(c. 480–400 BC)* — Founder of Buddhism

Frederick Buechner *(b. 1926)* — American writer and minister

Peter Buffett *(b. 1958)* — American musician, composer, author, and philanthropist

Warren Buffett *(b. 1930)* — American business magnate, investor, and philanthropist

Edmund Burke *(1729–1797)* — Irish statesman, orator, and philosopher

John Burroughs *(1837–1921)* — American naturalist and essayist

Leo Buscaglia *(1924–1998)* — American writer, motivational speaker, and professor

Saffron Burrows *(b. 1972)* — British actress

Barbara Bush *(b. 1925)* — former first lady of the United States and humanitarian

Candace Bushnell *(b. 1958)* — American novelist

Samuel Butler *(1835–1902)* — British novelist and writer

Albert Camus *(1913–1960)* — French novelist, essayist, and dramatist

Truman Capote *(1924–1984)* — American novelist, screenwriter, playwright, and actor

Dale Carnegie *(1888–1955)* — American writer and lecturer

Emily Carr *(1871–1945)* — Canadian artist and writer

David Carradine *(1936–2009)* — American actor and martial artist

Lewis Carroll *(1832–1898)* — British writer, mathematician, and photographer

Johnny Carson *(1925–2005)* — American television host, comedian, writer, producer, and actor

George Washington Carver *(1860–1943)* — American botanist, inventor, and educator

Michael Chabon *(b. 1963)* — American writer

Marc Chagall *(1887–1985)* — Russian-born French artist

Coco Chanel *(1883–1971)* — French fashion designer

Malcolm de Chazal *(1902–1981)* — Mauritian writer, painter, and visionary

John Cheever *(1912–1982)* — American writer

Anton Chekhov *(1860–1904)* — Russian dramatist and writer

G.K. Chesterton *(1874–1936)* — British journalist, novelist, and essayist

Julia Child *(1912–2004)* — American chef, author, and television personality

Deepak Chopra *(b. 1947)* — Indian-born American author and public speaker

Agatha Christie *(1890–1976)* — British novelist, playwright, and poet

Winston Churchill *(1874–1965)* — British statesman and prime minister

Dick Clark *(1929–2012)* — American game show host, businessman, and radio and television personality

John Cleese *(b. 1939)* — British actor, comedian, screenwriter, and producer

Jackie Collins *(1937–2015)* — British-born American romance novelist

Joan Collins *(b. 1933)* — British actress, author, and columnist

Charles Caleb Colton *(1780–1832)* — British cleric, writer, and collector

Confucius *(551–479 BC)* — Chinese philosopher

Noël Coward *(1899–1973)* — British playwright, composer, director, actor, and singer

e.e. cummings *(1894–1962)* — American poet

Anna Cummins *(b. 1980)* — American gold-medal Olympic rower

Salvador Dalí *(1904–1989)* — Spanish artist

Charles Darwin *(1809–1882)* — British naturalist, geologist, and author

Bette Davis *(1908–1989)* — American actress

Karen DeCrow *(1937–2014)* — American journalist, attorney, and author

Agnes de Mille *(1905–1993)* — American dancer and choreographer

John Dewey *(1859–1952)* — American philosopher, psychologist, and educator

Emily Dickinson *(1830–1886)* — American poet

Marlene Dietrich *(1901–1992)* — German actress and singer

Annie Dillard *(b. 1945)* — American writer

Walt Disney *(1901–1966)* — American cartoonist, film producer, and entrepreneur

Benjamin Disraeli *(1804–1881)* — British politician, writer, and prime minister

Mike Ditka *(b. 1939)* — American football player, coach, and television commentator

Fyodor Dostoevsky *(1821–1881)* — Russian novelist, journalist, and philosopher

Frederick Douglass *(1818–1895)* — American abolitionist, author, and diplomat

Rita Dove *(b. 1952)* — American poet and author

Theodore Dreiser *(1871–1945)* — American author

Henry Drummond *(1851–1897)* — Scottish evangelist, writer, and lecturer

Isadora Duncan *(1877–1927)* — American dancer and choreographer

Will Durant *(1885–1981)* — American historian, writer, and philosopher

Bob Dylan *(b. 1941)* — American singer and songwriter

Clint Eastwood *(b. 1930)* — American actor, film producer and director, and politician

Marie von Ebner-Eschenbach *(1830–1916)* — Austrian writer and essayist

Thomas A. Edison *(1847–1931)* — American inventor

Albert Einstein *(1879–1955)* — German-born American physicist

T.S. Eliot *(1888–1965)* — American-born English poet, writer, and critic

Duke Ellington *(1899–1974)* — American bandleader, musician, and composer

Ralph Waldo Emerson *(1803–1882)* — American essayist and poet

Enya *(b. 1961)* — Irish singer, songwriter, and musician

Epictetus *(c. 55–135 AD)* — Greek philosopher

Desiderius Erasmus *(1466–1536)* — Dutch priest, social critic, teacher, and theologian

Euripides *(480–406 BC)* — Greek playwright

Federico Fellini *(1920–1993)* — Italian film director and screenwriter

F. Scott Fitzgerald *(1896–1940)* — American writer

Gustave Flaubert *(1821–1880)* — French writer

Malcolm Forbes *(1919–1990)* —American publisher and business leader

Henry Ford *(1863–1947)* — American industrialist and founder of the Ford Motor Company

E.M. Forster *(1879–1970)* — British writer

Michael J. Fox *(b. 1961)* — Canadian-born American actor, author, and disabilities activist

Anatole France *(1844–1924)* — French poet, journalist, and novelist

Anne Frank *(1929–1945)* — German diarist

Benjamin Franklin *(1706–1790)* — American statesman and philosopher

Betty Friedan *(1921–2006)* — American writer and feminist

Robert Frost *(1874–1963)* — American poet

Neil Gaiman *(b. 1960)* — British author

Juan Pablo Galavis *(b. 1981)* — American-born Venezuelan soccer player and reality television star

Galileo Galilei *(1564–1642)* — Italian astronomer, physicist, engineer, philosopher, and mathematician

Mahatma Gandhi *(1869–1948)* — Indian nationalist leader

Hamlin Garland *(1860–1940)* — American poet, novelist, and parapsychology researcher

Shakti Gawain *(b. 1948)* — American writer and publisher

Frank Gehry *(b. 1929)* — Canadian-born architect

Theodor Geisel (a.k.a. Dr. Seuss) *(1904–1991)* — American writer, cartoonist, animator, publisher, and artist

Khalil Gibran *(1883–1931)* — Lebanese novelist, poet, and artist

Ellen Glasgow *(1873–1945)* — American novelist

John Glenn *(b. 1921)* — American astronaut, engineer, and US Senator

Elinor Glyn *(1864–1943)* — British novelist and scriptwriter

Seth Godin *(b. 1960)* — American author and entrepreneur

William Godwin *(1756–1836)* — British journalist, philosopher, and novelist

Johann Wolfgang von Goethe *(1749–1832)* — German poet and dramatist

Andy Goldsworthy *(b. 1956)* — British sculptor and photographer

Martha Graham *(1894–1991)* — American dancer and choreographer

Graham Greene *(1904–1991)* — British writer

Hafiz of Persia *(c. 1325–1389)* — Persian poet

Conrad Hall *(1926–2003)* — Polynesian-born American cinematographer

G. Stanley Hall *(1844–1924)* — American psychologist and educator

Mia Hamm *(b. 1972)* — American soccer player

Darell Hammond *(b. 1971)* — American philanthropist

Thich Nhat Hanh *(b. 1926)* — Vietnamese Buddhist monk, peace activist, and writer

Tom Hanks *(b. 1956)* — American actor and filmmaker

Mata Hari *(1876–1917)* — Dutch exotic dancer, courtesan, and suspected spy

Sydney J. Harris *(1917–1986)* — American journalist and author

Nathaniel Hawthorne *(1804–1864)* — American novelist

Helen Hayes *(1900–1993)* — American actress

Jimi Hendrix *(1942–1970)* — American rock musician and songwriter

Audrey Hepburn *(1929–1993)* — British actress and humanitarian

Hesiod *(c. 750–650 BC)* — Greek poet

Lou Holtz *(b. 1937)* — American football player and coach

Jane Howard *(1935–1996)* — American writer and journalist

E.W. Howe *(1853–1937)* — American novelist and editor

Elbert Hubbard *(1856–1915)* — American writer, publisher, and artist

Langston Hughes *(1902–1967)* — American poet, dramatist, and social activist

Zora Neale Hurston *(1891–1960)* — American writer, folklorist, and anthropologist

Robert M. Hutchins *(1899–1977)* — American university president and philosopher

Thomas Huxley *(1825–1895)* — British zoologist

Ada Louise Huxtable *(1921–2013)* — American architecture critic

Ice-T *(b. 1958)* — American musician and actor

Eric Idle *(b. 1943)* — British actor, composer, musician, and writer

Eugene Ionesco *(1909–1994)* — Romanian playwright

Helen Hunt Jackson *(1830–1885)* — American poet and writer

Henry James *(1811–1882)* — American philosopher

Thomas Jefferson *(1743–1826)* — Third president of the United States

Steve Jobs *(1955–2011)* — American entrepreneur, inventor, and co-founder, chairman, and CEO of Apple, Inc.

Billy Joel *(b. 1949)* — American singer-songwriter, composer, and pianist

Samuel Johnson *(1709–1784)* — British essayist, poet, and lexicographer

Michael Jordan *(b. 1963)* — American basketball player, businessman, and writer

Henry J. Kaiser *(1882–1967)* — American industrialist

Jon Katz *(b. 1947)* — American journalist, author, and photographer

Danny Kaye *(1911–1987)* — American actor, singer, dancer, and comedian

John Keats *(1795–1821)* — British poet

Garrison Keillor *(b. 1942)* — American author, storyteller, and radio personality

Helen Keller *(1880–1968)* — American writer, activist, and educator

Rose Kennedy *(1890–1995)* — American philanthropist

Jack Kerouac *(1922–1969)* — American journalist, novelist, and poet

John Maynard Keynes *(1883–1946)* — British economist

Omar Khayyam *(1048–1131)* — Persian mathematician, astronomer, philosopher, and poet

Harmon Killebrew *(1936–2011)* — American baseball player

Martin Luther King, Jr. *(1929–1968)* — American clergyman and civil rights leader

Barbara Kingsolver *(b. 1955)* — American writer

Paul Klee *(1879–1940)* — Swiss painter

Jeff Koons *(b. 1955)* — American artist

Jiddu Krishnamurti *(1895–1986)* — Indian writer and speaker

Anne Lamott *(b. 1954)* — American writer

Walter Savage Landor *(1775–1864)* — British poet and author

Doug Larson *(b. 1926)* — American journalist

Christopher Lasch *(1932–1994)* — historian and social critic

D.H. Lawrence *(1885–1930)* — British novelist and poet

Bruce Lee *(1940–1973)* — Chinese-American martial artist and actor

Ursula K. Le Guin *(b. 1929)* — American novelist

John Lennon *(1940–1980)* — English musician, singer, writer, record producer, and social activist

Doris Lessing *(1919–2013)* — English writer

C.S. Lewis *(1898–1963)* — Irish-born British novelist and essayist

Abraham Lincoln *(1809–1865)* — Sixteenth president of the United States

Charles Lindbergh *(1902–1974)* — American aviator, author, and inventor

Henry Wadsworth Longfellow *(1807–1882)* — American poet

John Lubbock *(1834–1913)* — British politician, scientist, and philanthropist

Gustav Mahler *(1860–1911)* — Austrian composer and conductor

Nelson Mandela *(1918–2013)* — South African political leader, activist, humanitarian, and lawyer

Horace Mann *(1796–1859)* — American educator and politician

Julianna Margulies *(b. 1966)* — American actress and producer

Christopher Marlowe *(1564–1593)* — British playwright and poet

Groucho Marx *(1890–1977)* — American comedian and film and television star

Karl Marx *(1818–1883)* — Prussian-born German philosopher, economist, and journalist

Henri Matisse *(1869–1954)* — French artist

André Maurois *(1885–1967)* — French writer

Phil McGraw *(b. 1950)* — American psychologist, author, and television host

Mignon McLaughlin *(1913–1983)* — American journalist and author

Bernard Meltzer *(1916–1998)* — American radio host

Joyce Meyer *(b. 1943)* — American author and speaker

Edna St. Vincent Millay *(1892–1950)* — American poet

Henry Miller *(1891–1980)* — American writer

Molière *(1622–1673)* — French playwright and actor

Marilyn Monroe *(1926–1962)* — American actress and model

Thomas S. Monson *(b. 1927)* — religious leader and author

Ashley Montagu *(1905–1999)* — British-born American anthropologist

Maria Montessori *(1870–1952)* — Italian physician and educator

L.M. Montgomery *(1874–1942)* — Canadian writer

Jeanne Moreau *(b. 1928)* — French actress and director

John Muir *(1838–1914)* — Scottish-born American naturalist

Randall Munroe *(b. 1984)* — American cartoonist and author

Haruki Murakami *(b. 1949)* — Japanese writer

Iris Murdoch *(1919–1999)* — British writer

Vladimir Nabokov *(1899–1977)* — Russian-born American novelist

George Jean Nathan *(1882–1958)* — American drama critic and editor

Gloria Naylor *(b. 1950)* — American novelist

Pablo Neruda *(1904–1973)* — Chilean poet and diplomat

Jack Nicholson *(b. 1937)* — American actor and filmmaker

Friedrich Nietzsche *(1844–1900)* — German philosopher

Henri Nouwen *(1932–1996)* — Dutch priest, professor, and writer

Sean O'Casey *(1880–1964)* — Irish playwright

Mary Oliver *(b. 1935)* — American poet

James Oppenheim *(1882–1932)* — American poet, novelist, and editor

Susan Orlean *(b. 1955)* — American journalist and author

Ovid *(43 BC–17 AD)* — Roman poet

Cynthia Ozick *(b. 1928)* — American writer

Violeta Parra *(1917–1967)* — Chilean composer, ethnomusicologist, and artist

Norman Vincent Peale *(1898–1993)* — American author, minister, and public speaker

Pablo Picasso *(1881–1973)* — Spanish artist

Brad Pitt *(b. 1963)* — American actor and producer

Plato *(c. 428–348 BC)* — Greek philosopher and writer

Roman Polanski *(b. 1933)* — French film director, writer, and actor

Alexander Pope *(1688–1744)* — English poet

Katherine Anne Porter *(1890–1980)* — American writer

Natalie Portman *(b. 1981)* — Israeli-born American actress

Marcel Proust *(1871–1922)* — French novelist

Ayn Rand *(1905–1982)* — Russian-born American novelist and philosopher

Rachel Naomi Remen *(b. 1938)* — author, professor, and leader in integrative medicine

Ernest Renan *(1823–1892)* — French philosopher, historian, and writer

Jules Renard *(1864–1910)* — French author

Tom Robbins *(b. 1932)* — American writer

Will Rogers *(1879–1935)* — American comedian, writer, and radio personality

Henry Rollins *(b. 1961)* — American musician, journalist, actor, and artist

Eleanor Roosevelt *(1884–1962)* — American humanitarian, political activist, and longest-serving First Lady of the United States

Theodore Roosevelt *(1858–1919)* — Twenty-sixth president of the United States

Jean Rostand *(1894–1977)* — French biologist

Theodore Rubin *(b. 1923)* — American psychiatrist and author

Rumi *(1207–1273)* — Persian poet and religious scholar

John Ruskin *(1819–1900)* — British writer, critic, and artist

Babe Ruth *(1895–1948)* — American baseball player

Antoine de Saint-Exupéry *(1900–1944)* — French writer, poet, and aviator

George Sand *(1804–1876)* — French writer

Carl Sandburg *(1878–1967)* — American poet and journalist

Friedrich Schiller *(1759–1805)* — German poet, writer, historian, and philosopher

Charles M. Schulz *(1922–2000)* — American cartoonist

Amy Schumer *(b. 1981)* — American comedian, actress, and producer

Albert Schweitzer *(1875–1965)* — German-born French theologian, humanitarian, and doctor

Seneca *(4 BC–65 AD)* — Roman philosopher and playwright

Thomas Shadwell *(c. 1642–1692)* — British poet and playwright

William Shakespeare *(1564–1616)* — British playwright, poet, and actor

William Shatner *(b. 1931)* — Canadian actor, producer, and advertising spokesman

George Bernard Shaw *(1856–1950)* — Irish playwright and author

Percy Bysshe Shelley *(1792–1822)* — British poet, novelist, and playwright

Brooke Shields *(b. 1965)* — American actress and model

Bernie Siegel *(b. 1932)* — American writer and surgeon

Shel Silverstein *(1930–1999)* — American writer, poet, cartoonist, and playwright

Neil Simon *(b. 1927)* — American playwright and writer

Dodie Smith *(1896–1990)* — British novelist and playwright

C.P. Snow *(1905–1980)* — British physical chemist and writer

Socrates *(c. 470–399 BC)* — Greek philosopher

Solon *(c. 638–558 BC)* — Greek lawmaker and poet

Aleksandr Solzhenitsyn *(1918–2008)* — Russian writer

Sonia Sotomayor *(b. 1954)* — American Supreme Court Justice

Lincoln Steffens *(1866–1936)* — American journalist

John Steinbeck *(1902–1968)* — American writer

Casey Stengel *(1890–1975)* — American baseball player and manager

Wallace Stevens *(1879–1955)* — American poet

Robert Louis Stevenson *(1850–1894)* — Scottish writer

Sly Stone *(b. 1943)* — American musician

Tom Stoppard *(b. 1937)* — Czech-born British playwright

Igor Stravinsky *(1882–1971)* — Russian-born composer, pianist, and conductor

Keith Sweat *(b. 1961)* — American singer-songwriter and record producer

Jonathan Swift *(1667–1745)* — Irish writer

Taylor Swift *(b. 1989)* — American singer-songwriter

Charles R. Swindoll *(b. 1934)* — American author, educator, and pastor

Publilius Syrus *(c. 85–43 BC)* — Syrian-born Roman writer

Edward Teller *(1908–2003)* — Hungarian-born American physicist

Alfred Lord Tennyson *(1809–1892)* — British poet

Mother Teresa *(1910–1997)* — Albanian-born Roman Catholic nun, declared Blessed in 2003, who devoted her life to the poor of Calcutta

Twyla Tharp *(b. 1941)* — American dancer and choreographer

Paul Theroux *(b. 1941)* — American writer and critic

Dylan Thomas *(1914–1953)* — Welsh poet and writer

Henry David Thoreau *(1817–1862)* — American writer and philosopher

Leo Tolstoy *(1828–1910)* — Russian writer

Arnold J. Toynbee *(1889–1975)* — British historian

Mark Twain *(1835–1910)* — American writer and lecturer

Lao Tzu *(c. sixth century BC)* — Chinese poet and philosopher

Brenda Ueland *(1891–1985)* — American journalist and writer

John Updike *(1932–2009)* — American writer

J.J. Van Der Leeuw *(1893–1934)* — Dutch author and theosophist

Henry Van Dyke *(1852–1933)* — American writer and educator

Vincent van Gogh *(1853–1890)* — Dutch artist

Leonardo da Vinci *(1452–1519)* — Italian artist, scientist, writer, historian, and architect

David Viscott *(1938–1996)* — American psychiatrist, author, and media personality

Alice Walker *(b. 1944)* — American writer and political activist

Booker T. Washington *(1856–1915)* — American educator, writer, and African-American leader

Kerry Washington *(b. 1977)* — American actress

Martha Washington *(1731–1802)* — First First Lady of the United States

Bill Watterson *(b. 1958)* — American cartoonist

Edith Wharton *(1862–1937)* — American writer

E.B. White *(1899–1985)* — American writer

Paul Dudley White *(1886–1973)* — American physician

Theodore White *(1915–1986)* — American journalist and historian

Walt Whitman *(1819–1892)* — American poet

Oscar Wilde *(1854–1900)* — Irish writer

Robin Williams *(1951–2014)* — American actor and comedian

E.O. Wilson *(b. 1929)* — American biologist and author

Woodrow Wilson *(1856–1924)* — Twenty-eighth president of the United States

Oprah Winfrey *(b. 1954)* — American media mogul, talk-show host, actress, and philanthropist

John Wooden *(1910–2010)* — American basketball player and coach

William Wordsworth *(1770–1850)* — British poet

Frank Lloyd Wright *(1867–1959)* — American architect

Andrew Wyeth *(1917–2009)* — American artist

William Butler Yeats *(1865–1939)* — Irish poet and playwright

Yevgeny Yevtushenko *(b. 1932)* — Russian poet, novelist, actor, and director

Loretta Young *(1913–2000)* — American actress

Malala Yousafzai *(b. 1997)* — Pakistani activist for the education of girls and youngest recipient of the Nobel Prize

Lin Yutang *(1895–1976)* — Chinese writer and inventor